ISBN 978-1-5281-5509-0
PIBN 10924033

1 MONTH OF
FREE
READING

at
www.ForgottenBooks.com

By purchasing this book you are eligible for one month membership to ForgottenBooks.com, giving you unlimited access to our entire collection of over 1,000,000 titles via our web site and mobile apps.

To claim your free month visit:
www.forgottenbooks.com/free924033

PROCEEDINGS REPORT
OF THE

BLACK WOMEN'S AGENDA, INC.
FOURTEENTH ANNUAL WORKSHOP

BLACK WOMEN IN CRISIS

Mobilizing Black Women
To Prevent and Reduce The Spread of
H.I.V. Disease

Grant Support Provided By
Office of Minority Health, DHHS
A Seminar Entitled
"AIDS and The Effects of HIV on Black Women and Girls"
#91AFO55277

September 13, 1991
Washington, D.C.

TABLE OF CONTENTS

Page

Presentations

THE BLACK WOMEN'S AGENDA, INC.

The Black Women's Agenda, Inc. (BWA) is a private non-profit volunteer organization dedicated to address, protect and advance the needs and rights of black women and girls in a constantly changing society. Established in 1977, BWA fulfills this mission exclusively through research, dissemination of information, education, training and advocacy. BWA's constituency comprises professional black women whose individual expertise and experiences are augmented by their membership in other established national women's organizations. Thus, BWA had formed a viable national coalition of black women's organizations. Accordingly, BWA has developed into a "think tank" with extensive national networking, outreach and information dissemination capabilities.

The History of The Black Women's Agenda

The Black Women's Agenda evolved from the work of ten women who responded to an urgent call to recognize and articulate the needs of black women within the women's movement by developing a Black Women's Action Plan. This plan was enthusiastically embraced by the black delegates to the International Women's Year (IWY) Conference in Houston, Texas in 1977. The plan became the basis for a resolution for minority women's rights and was adopted overwhelmingly by the 2,000 delegates in an emotionally charged atmosphere of togetherness.

Determined not to lose the momentum of the International Women's Year, the ten women formed an active organization in the nation's capital to support the recommendations in the Black Women's Action Plan. In September of 1978, 43 leaders of black women's organizations met with the ten women on Capitol Hill and pledged their support for the mission and program of what is now the Black Women's Agenda.

In June of 1979, BWA organized its first workshop in Washington. Since that date, BWA has held town meetings for U.S. Presidential candidates, symposia on racism and sexism, and annual workshops focused on priority issues.

BWA Implementation Strategies

To accomplish its mission, the Black Women's Agenda:

- Works for the elimination of racism;
- Advocates on Capitol Hill for black women everywhere;
- Tracks legislation and trends to recommend public policy changes to benefit black women and their families;
- Conducts public workshops and seminars, highlighting economic, social and civil liberty issues of black women and girls; and
- Conducts research and publishes papers and reports which assess the status and concerns of black women and girls.

Black Women's Agenda, Inc.
208 Auburn Avenue, N.E., Atlanta, GA 30303 Telephone (404) 524-8279

FOREWORD

The Black Women's Agenda since 1977 has mobilized women's groups for action on "cutting edge" challenges. Following in this tradition, this workshop seminar reflects BWA's commitment to address important issues which affect the lives of black women and their children. We can think of no issue more crucial or vital to the health of black women and their families than the effects on them of AIDS (Acquired Immune Deficiency Syndrome) and HIV (Human Immunodeficiency Virus) infection. We issued the call convening our members, supporters and sister organizations across the nation so that we might address together this growing health crisis.

Traditionally, many of us have felt that this is not an issue that affects the black community, and particularly not the middle class black community. We have found that this is certainly untrue. Our panelists, all of them, were eloquent in stating that AIDS and HIV infection are no respecters of class or educational level. We are all vulnerable. We are also all responsible for removing this scourge from our community and for aiding and comforting its victims.

We are compelled to action by these facts:
- Women are the fastest growing population to become infected with the virus.
- AIDS is the leading cause of death in New York and New Jersey among African American women of child-bearing age.
- Women tend to die faster than men once they are diagnosed with AIDS.
- African American women are nine times more likely to die of AIDS than white women.
- Black women comprise 12.6 percent of the population, but 52 percent of all women with AIDS.
- In a recent poll, 84 percent of African women did not believe they are at risk of contacting AIDS.

We convened this workshop seminar not only to talk about what the disease is, what the infection is, and how it affects us, but also how we can affect this health emergency in a positive way. The crisis is real and the challenge is enormous. Still Black women have a heritage of facing impossible odds and overcoming them. It is important to remind ourselves that we are powerful, not powerless. We have a responsibility to learn all we can, to take information back to our communities, and to take action to put AIDS and HIV infection on everyone's agenda.

"Everyone to whom much is given, of him will much be required." Let us go forth and make a difference in our world. Our people desperately need us.

Dolly D. Adams
President

"BLACK WOMEN IN CRISIS"

MOBILIZING BLACK WOMEN TO PREVENT AND REDUCE THE SPREAD OF H.I.V. DISEASE

WORKSHOP OBJECTIVES

I. Bring together the collective leadership of black women's organizations and representatives of community and neighborhood groups and individuals who are committed to working actively for adequate health care for black women, in order to increase awareness of the devastation of AIDS and HIV infection in the black community and how the black woman is targeted by the disease.

II. Ascertain the level of involvement by organizations, groups, and individuals in the prevention, education and treatment of those women at risk, vulnerable women and those with the infection.

III. Plan strategies for the heretofore unreached to involve them in the struggle.

IV. Provide information about effective models and concrete strategies already operating in black communities.

V. Encourage through our interaction the beginning and/or continuing participation in advocacy at the city and state level for clinics, hospital services, outreach programs, and the planning and execution of educational programs at the neighborhood level.

VI. Document the results of this workshop which will provide a "pulse reading" of the progress and barriers to AIDS education, access to health care, medical treatment, clinical trials, public support and family bonding.

VII. Mobilize the collective leadership of black women's organizations, community groups and health activists in establishing a Work Plan that sets a timetable for developing an action strategy and setting goals.

Participating Organizations

Alpha Kappa Alpha Sorority
Delta Sigma Theta Sorority
Jack & Jill of America, Inc.
International Women's Department of The Church of God in Christ
Iota Phi Lambda Sorority, Inc.
National Association of Black Women Attorneys
National Association of Colored Women's Clubs
National Association of Media Women
National Association of Negro Business & Professional Women's Clubs
Sigma Gamma Rho Sorority
The Links, Inc.
The Women's Auxiliary to the National Baptist Convention of America
Women's Auxiliary of Progressive National Baptist Church
Women's Home and Overseas Missionary Society of the A.M.E. Zion Church
Women's Missionary Council of the C.M.E. Church
Women's Missionary Society of the A.M.E. Church
Zeta Phi Beta Sorority, Inc.

MEET THE PRESENTERS

Margaret Joan Cousin, Supervisor, Women's Missionary Society of the A.M.E. Church, Eleventh Episcopal District

Margaret Joan Cousin, Supervisor of the Women's Missionary Society for the Eleventh Episcopal District, has been in the forefront of efforts to involve women of the African Methodist Episcopal (A.M.E.) Church in programs that respond to human needs. As the result of her efforts, AIDS Stations have been established in A.M.E. churches across the state of Florida. These "stations" are designed to help meet spiritual, psychological, physical and social needs of AIDS patients, and serve as educational centers for aiding families of AIDS patients. They also provide information to community residents about the disease and how to avoid it.

Mrs. Cousin is a graduate of Central State College in Wilberforce, Ohio. She is the recipient of Rockefeller grants for study at Duke University, Cornell University and institutions of higher learning in Ghana and Nigeria in West Africa. An educator, she developed the curriculum for the study of African American history for the Department of Public Instruction in Raleigh, North Carolina. She also organized the Sarah Allen House in Miami, Florida, which provides housing and services to the poor and homeless in that city.

Mrs. Cousin is a member of the Executive Board of the Duval County AIDS and Substance Abuse Center, as well as many other church and civic groups.

Rashidah L. Hassan, Co-Founder and Chief Executive Officer, BEBASHI (Blacks Educating Blacks About Sexual Health Issues)

Rashidah Lorraine Hassan directs BEBASHI, one of the largest independent community-based education programs in the country. A registered nurse and certified Infection Control Practitioner, Ms. Hassan created BEBASHI to get across the message that AIDS threatens everyone, especially people of color, not only in Philadelphia, but nationally and internationally as well. BEBASHI informs people of the life-threatening consequences of risky sexual behavior and drug abuse, and teaches them practical ways to protect themselves.

Respected for her innovative approach to public health education, she has developed "down-to-earth" strategies for educating people about HIV infection, syphilis and other sexually transmitted diseases. Previous positions include service as a Coordinator of Infection Control Programs and Head Nurse at Albert Einstein Medical Center, and Nursing Clinical Coordinator at Cedars-Sinai in Los Angeles. She also served as Infection Control Nurse Epidemiologist at the Philadelphia Department of Public Health Division of Communicable Disease. Mrs. Hassan is a graduate of the Medical College of Pennsylvania and LaSalle University.

Mrs. Hassan is actively involved in many community and professional organizations. For example, she is a board member of the National Minority AIDS Council, The Philadelphia AIDS Consortium, and the Community Advisory Board of the Center for

Disease Control, Atlanta, GA. She is also on the faculty of the Family Planning Council of Southeastern Pennsylvania Ob/Gyn Nurse Practitioners Training Program.

Toni Miles-Maloney, Community Program Director, March of Dimes, National Capital Area Chapter.

Toni Miles-Maloney holds a Bachelor of Science in health education and public health administration from the University of the District of Columbia. In her current role, she carries the message of AIDS and HIV infection prevention to audiences of all ages. Before assuming her current responsibilities, she served as Health Services Liaison for Howard University's AIDS Minority Infrastructure Program. She provided state-of-the art HIV information to local health care providers working with minority patients, and shared HIV education and counseling for patients referred for clinical studies.

Other outreach and public education assignments included service as Project Director of the Beautiful Babies Project; coordination of the D.C. Public Schools HIV/AIDS Education Instructional Program; and assistance with direct patient care at the Hillcrest Women's Surgi-Center.

In these roles Ms. Miles-Maloney developed and marketed videos, established and maintained a library of current AIDS information materials, and conducted in-service educational sessions for clinical personnel. She also coordinated DCPS HIV/AIDS activities for youth, serving as the liaison for student peer educators and their parents.

Celia J. Maxwell, M.D., Director of HUMED Travel Medicine, Associate Director of the HIV Service, Howard University Hospital

Dr. Celia Maxwell's practice consists primarily of the treatment of tropical and infectious diseases. In addition to maintaining responsibility for 700 AIDS and HIV infected patients and her dual directing assignments at the university, she is a co-investigator for a federal grant to establish an AIDS Clinical Trials Unit at Howard University.

Dr. Maxwell obtained a medical degree from the Columbia University College of Physicians and Surgeons after first securing a Bachelors Degree in Nursing from Hunter College. After completing internship and residency training in Internal Medicine at Howard University Hospital, she was awarded a Fellowship in Parasitology at the National Institutes of Health, Laboratory of Parasitic Diseases. Having completed the fellowship, she returned to Howard University as an Infectious Disease Fellow and was subsequently appointed Assistant Professor of Medicine.

She has given numerous talks to scientific and lay audiences alike and has several publications on sexually transmitted diseases and parasitology to her credit. In November 1990, she was named by Mayor-elect Sharon Pratt Dixon to co-chair the Transitional Task Force on AIDS services. A native of Panama, Dr. Maxwell is bilingual, board certified and a fellow of the American College of Physicians.

Frances E. Page, Policy Analyst, National Commission on AIDS

Frances Page's career involves 20 years of nursing and 15 years of health education experience. In her present position, she has responsibility for Commission activities, including community presentations, responding to requests for information and preparing policy documents. She formerly served as Program Manager for the National AIDS Minority Information and Education Program of Howard University's College of Medicine, a national program funded by the Center for Disease Control. She was also responsible for health education and promotion regarding AIDS for Enterprises for New Directions.

Holder of both B.S. and Master's degrees in public health from the University of South Carolina, Ms. Page has also served as Supervisor of the Infection Control Office and as Nurse Epidemiologist for Howard University Hospital. She served as Co-Chair for the Train-the Trainer Subcommittee for D.C. AIDS Educators. As a consultant for the Youth Awareness Program, she held classes for teens on such topics as value judgments, pregnancy and sexually transmitted diseases.

She has also held supervisory, teaching and "front-line" nursing positions at the University of South Carolina, Prince Georges General Hospital and in West Berlin, Germany. An active participant in community activities, Ms. Page advises the federal government as a member of the National Strategic Committee for AIDS in the African American Communities for the Office of Minority Health and is a member of the HIV/AIDS Training Institute Advisory Panel for the Health Resources and Services Administration.

Julia R. Scott, Director, National Black Women's Health Project (NBWHP), Public Policy and Education Office

Julia R. Scott is a registered nurse and graduate of the Waterbury Hospital School of Nursing, and is a Certified Family Planning Nurse Practitioner. She is responsible for public education and outreach, management, planning and policy-related activities for the D.C. Office of NBWHP. This Atlanta-based organization is a national program of self-help and health advocacy that develops and administers programs to empower African American women and to bring about a more equitable distribution of health care resources.

Previous assignments included coordination of Child Watch for the Children's Defense Fund, a national project which networks with Black, Hispanic and other organizations, and provides support to volunteers for action plans to prevent children having children. She also held several leadership positions with the Ms. Foundation for Women, Inc., a national foundation devoted to enhancing the status of women.

In the area of community and direct service, Ms. Page has been a Director and Nurse Practitioner at a community service agency delivering comprehensive services. She also served as Training Director for the Boston Family Planning Project and has been a head nurse/team leader for several health institutions in the state of Massachusetts.

Leslie R. Wolfe, Ph.D., Executive Director,
Center for Women Policy Studies

Dr. Leslie Wolfe has served since 1987 as Executive Director of the Center, a Washington-based national feminist policy and advocacy organization founded in 1972. Previously, she directed the Project on Equal Education Rights of the NOW Legal Defense and Education Fund and the Women's Educational Equity Act Program in the U.S. Department of Education. She also served as Deputy Director of the Women's Rights Program for the U.S. Commission on Civil Rights.

Dr. Wolfe has consulted widely, providing management and program development services to national nonprofit organizations such as the Federation of Organizations for Professional Women, Women's Lobby, Inc. and the National Welfare Rights Organization.

Her civic involvement is extensive. She chairs the Board of Directors of The Children's Foundation, is a member of the Board of the National Council for Research on Women and serves on the Montgomery County (MD) Commission for Women. She also advises the Women's Economic Justice Center of the Center for Policy Alternatives. She has a number of publications to her credit, addressing such topics as educational equity, feminism, curriculum development, women and sports.

EXECUTIVE SUMMARY

"Sisters, we need to be there!" From opening remarks by Dr. Dolly D. Adams to the final burst of applause from the audience, being there, bringing information, aid and comfort to persons in the black community infected and affected by AIDS was a much echoed refrain.

The occasion was the Black Women's Agenda Fourteenth Annual Workshop, "Black Women in Crisis." Consistent with the seminar's official title, "AIDS and the Effect of HIV on Black Women and Girls," presenters gave extensive documentation of AIDS/HIV as a medical, statistical and socio-economic phenomenon. In accordance with the workshop's action title, "Mobilizing Black Women to Prevent and Reduce the Spread of HIV Disease," Black Women's Agenda, Inc. (BWA) also presented speakers who could challenge, motivate and inspire workshop participants to get involved.

The workshop alternated between rally and revival, camp meeting and classroom. Yet all of the speakers, whatever their style of delivery, were of one accord regarding the message to be shared. "AIDS threatens the black community's survival. AIDS/HIV can infect and affects all of us. This disease is everyone's concern, and there is something each of us can do to prevent and reduce its spread, and to aid its victims."

The welcome issued by Dr. Adams, National President of BWA, set the tone for the morning's proceedings. She told the audience of approximately 300 women and men that the purpose of the workshop/seminar was: "not only to talk about what the disease is, what the infection is, how it affects us, but also...how we can affect it in a positive way."

This message, that there is something black women can do about the AIDS, was echoed by Mrs. Etta Moten Barnett, who at ninety is the senior member of the BWA Board of Directors. Mrs. Barnett stressed the role. of empowerment in bringing BWA to its current position of strength and its importance "as we prepare for the 21st century."

Dr. Delores L. K. Williams, another BWA board member and President of the Women's Missionary Society of the African Methodist Episcopal Church, further emphasized in her meditative remarks, the responsibility of black women to go forth and "make a difference." She reminded the audience: "Every one to whom much is given, of him will much be required."

Mrs. Maudine Cooper, Vice President for Legislation for BWA and President of the Washington Urban League, focused discussion on the seriousness of the AIDS/HIV disease and its impact on all women: "The one thing about AIDS that differs from all the other sexually transmitted diseases, is that the bottom line is death. It's death to our loved ones, death to our friends." She brought this point home by asking for a show of hands of all those in the room who had known at least one person who had died of AIDS. Approximately 65 percent of the audience responded affirmatively. Her conclusion was inescapable: "It's not a stranger; it's not a joke....It's a serious issue for black women."

Introductory remarks were shared by Dr. Lynette Taylor, former BWA President and

current board member, as she presented the representatives of national women's organizations invited to participate in the workshop. She sounded yet another theme. She spoke of the importance of "combining our resources" and the need for commitment to communication, service, networking, sharing and caring as prerequisites for successful collective effort.

Ms. Ethel James Williams, the workshop's moderator, was introduced by Dr. Bernadine Denning as the person most responsible for identifying and convening the panel experts. Ms. Williams warned participants that mobilization was urgently required ("It's ten minutes to midnight"), and then shared seven workshop objectives: 1) Bringing together activist organizations and individuals in order to increase awareness of AIDS/HIV infection, its devastation in the black community, particularly for black women; 2) ascertaining current levels of involvement with women at risk, those vulnerable and those with the infection; 3) planning strategies to involve those not yet reached; 4) providing information about operating models and concrete strategies; 5) encouraging advocacy for community services and programs at the neighborhood level; 6) documenting workshop results; and 7) mobilizing collective leadership in establishing work plans.

The first panelist, Mrs. Margaret Joan Cousin, Supervisor, Women's Missionary Society of the A.M.E. Church, Eleventh Episcopal District, asked her listeners to remove the cloak of "invisibility" that covers people living with AIDS. She urged her listeners to follow the example of churchmen and women in Florida who have gone to the hospitals to check on the babies born HIV positive. She told of visits to nursing homes and the Orange County Jail, where seven black women in the back, kept away from other prisoners, were told: "We love you. We're not afraid to touch you." Urging the audience to follow the path of Christain commitment, she urged them to be bold, committed and fearless in order to "prepare for the unborn...beyond the year 2000."

The presentation of Ms. Julia R. Scott, who is Director of the National Black Women's Health Project, Public Policy and Education Office, created a statistical backdrop of black women's health as a dimension of the health crisis facing the United States as a whole. No matter what the measure, whether life expectancy, hypertension, infant mortality, suicide, cervical cancer or diabetes, the status of African American women suffers in comparison with other population groups. Black women's health is further affected by discrimination and poverty. In addition, Ms. Scott reported, black women do not suffer from the same diseases in the same proportion as the majority white population.

Nationally, she continued, AIDS is one of the 10 leading causes of death in women of reproductive age. In New York and New Jersey, AIDS is the number one killer of African American women of reproductive age. An additional indicator of the crisis: fifty-two percent of women with AIDS are black. "Until we view this disease as one we all could encounter and have, and unless we apply appropriate remedies, it will remain an epidemic." Therefore, she concluded, the real struggle is "with our own families, friends, homes and churches to change the attitudes about who it is that is affected and who gets AIDS and HIV infection....It is not enough to listen and to learn. We must go back, teach others and participate in activism required of us to address the most deadly disease of the 21st century."

Ms. Frances E. Page, Policy Analyst with the National Commission on AIDS, maintained that AIDS "is by far the worst disease I have ever had to encounter in my professional life." She began by sharing reflections from HIV infected women in the form of several minidramas which helped to make the statistics come alive. She asserted that AIDS is the number one health crisis in this decade. She further pointed out that for every AIDS case, there are 50 persons who are infected by the virus. As of July 1991, there were 186,895 reported cases of AIDS in the U.S. Using the formula, there are 9,334,750 Americans infected and countless others affected by the virus.

Ms. Page also cited statistics that clearly documented the threat HIV poses to African American women. Noting that black women are nine times more likely to die of AIDS than white women, she asked: "What does this mean for the future of our race? HIV disease can potentially wipe us from the face of the earth. Sisters, we need to wake up."

Addressing the issue, "Not in my neighborhood. I don't know anyone infected", Ms. Page reported that in reality, AIDS can be found in every state of the union, particularly those states from which seminar participants came. Even a small number of cases can indicate, using the 50 to 1 formula, a large number of persons who are infected.

Returning to her premise that there are live human beings behind these numbers, Ms. Page shared once again comments from women infected and affected by AIDS, for example: "I know I'm going to die. I don't know when. But until then, I want to know somebody is going to be there when I turn around and say, 'Help me!'" She concluded: "Sisters, we need to be there."

The next speaker was Dr. Celia J. Maxwell, Director of HUMED Travel Medicine and Associate Director of the HIV Service at Howard University Hospital. She made her purpose clear from the outset: "I want to tell these ladies the facts." She began by posing the question: "Why is this happening? Black women are being infected who are not engaged in high risk behaviors. Blood infusions and blood products are safer. The issue is that HIV infection is now primarily a sexually transmitted disease."

Dr. Maxwell then proceeded to describe some of the conditions unique to women that might facilitate or increase the risk of getting infected. Abrasions of the vagina is one such condition, as well as genital ulcers, syphilis and herpes. There are also some risks associated with oral contraceptives and intercourse during menstrual period. Dr. Maxwell warned that contact with bisexual men who are HIV positive and have certain other physical problems poses a special risk for African American women.

HIV disease manifests differently in women than men. Few women get Kaposi's sarcoma. Because there is limited awareness of these differences, women with the virus may be missed and not diagnosed properly. The average life expectancy for women with AIDS seems much shorter than that of men, possibly because women get to the doctor later.

Dr. Maxwell also discussed possible interventions, strongly recommending peer education and frequent pap smears. Having personal knowledge of one's own HIV status has also proven to be effective in changing behavior. However, she cautioned against use of Nonoxynol-9 as a preventive measure. She concluded her presentation by urging her listeners to "take charge". "We need to

educate ourselves first so we can talk to our children. We shouldn't hide the facts....Finally...remember that...people who live in a glass house, should not be out there throwing stones."

Ms. Toni Miles-Maloney is Community Program Director, March of Dimes, National Capital Area Chapter. She shared five "L's" with her listeners as important tools for AID prevention education. These are Look, Learn, Listen, Level and Love. She gave special emphasis to leveling with young people, telling them in her words, "the true truth," and displayed items she uses in sex and AIDS education classes involving young audiences. She also urged women with granddaughters or even great-granddaughter to become informed so that they can talk with younger members of the family. She urged the audience to use sources such as magazines, to pick up information from the doctor. "If you are hesitant about sharing it with young people at home, leave it on their beds."

Ms. Miles-Maloney addressed the final "L" or Love, and charged workshop attendees to be "foot-soldiers for AIDS education." She too urged those present not to forget the women who are infected with the virus. She concluded her presentation by emphasizing the importance of networking, adding: "You just have no idea how strong we really are. And as black women, there is nothing in the world that we cannot do."

Mrs. Rashida L. Hassan is the Chief Executive Officer and Co-Founder of Blacks Educating Blacks About Sexual Health Issues (BEBASHI). She stirred the workshop audience, urging participants not to indulge themselves "in the myths created by other communities that are draped over us." She then undertook to "explode" some of those myths. She challenged the assumption that black community does not talk about homosexuality and asked: "You tell me what black gay men have been relegated to separate neighborhoods?"

She also refuted the myths that "our own sexuality is the problem with our people", and noted that recent action in Congress appeared to reflect that position, by transferring a vast amount of money associated with AIDS prevention and education to client services. She warned that if the black community allows this to happen, "This disease will remain indigenous in our community from time on in."

In countering this myth, Mrs. Hassan tells black communities all over the country: "You know how to educate. You know how to prepare and care for people with AIDS...When someone is dying, you comfort them. Nobody is doing that for us...That's our responsibility." She also disputed the myth that the church will not deal with AIDS or that the message of abstinence cannot be communicated to black youth effectively.

Returning to her essential message, "We must save ourselves," Mrs. Hassan urged black women to take responsibility for educating the community, for approaching policy makers and legislators, for getting the attention of the African American media, for holding prayer vigils, prayer marches and even "ugly demonstrations." People are also needed to raise funds, write proposals and develop care in the African American cultural context.

Predicting that AIDS would be moved to a forefront agenda if women moved it, she delivered this final challenge: "Come back home. We can deal with our own homelessness, our own poor education. We

have all we need as a nation, an African American nation, to do something about this epidemic. We cannot debate it. We need to just go out and do what has to be done."

Dr. Leslie Wolfe, Executive Director of the Center for Women Policy Studies, was the final presenter. Dr. Wolfe reiterated the point that the social and economic status of women is often ignored in policy discussions about HIV disease.

Asserting that AIDS affects not only women of childbearing age, but also young girls and women over 44, who "still have a life", she emphasized the point. "All of us are at risk."

She described pending pieces of legislation, including the Women and AIDS Outreach and Prevention Act, which would give funds to health care providers already serving low income women, and the Women and AIDS Research Initiative, which would require federal agencies to create women-focused AIDS research programs. Both bills have been introduced by U.S. Representative Contance Morella.

Dr. Wolfe urged that priority attention by given by those present to the Social Security and SSI AIDS Disability Act of 1991. This bill would require the Social Security Administration to use a different definition of HIV disability, one which would reflect awareness of HIV's effects and manifestations in women as well as men. Her final words served as an appropriate call to action. "We are not the problem; we are the creators of the solution. And we are the ones....who are taking the kind of leadership that will ensure that our federal government joins the communities of women, to fight for our sisters' lives and for our own."

PRESENTATION

"One Church's Response to AIDS in the Black Community"

--Margaret J. Cousin

Giving God the glory, Mrs. Cousin described her involvement in HIV education and AIDS projects since 1984. She shared with the audience that she had "prayed for the day to come when we can take this virus out of the closet and talk freely." She also sounded a clear note of warning: "If we don't do something, we won't be around to tell the story."

Choosing to focus not on people dying with AIDS, but rather on people living with AIDS, Mrs. Cousin described her experiences in Florida, beginning with a two year study in Jacksonville. She emphasized the need for Concern, Compassion, Care and Commitment, and urged her listeners to look at people. Noting that many persons with AIDS are treated like Ralph Ellison's "invisible man", she urged those assembled to "feel the compassion" and recognize that: "These are God's children." Her call to those following Christian teachings was to "move from being powerless to powerful. If we call ourselves the Church, we are the only physical bodies that can manifest what God is."

Mrs. Cousin reported that AIDS is epidemic in Florida. In 1988, Miami was number three in the country in HIV infection and number one in pediatric AIDS. Having been aware of this crisis for some time, she and the African Methodist Episcopal Women's Missionary Society have worked and investigated. In West Palm Beach there is a group that works with HIV babies. She urged the women present to find out what is happening to the babies who are born HIV positive. By the time the babies are 15 months old, they may be HIV free. "Yet, if we are not careful", she said, "they will be written off. We all need to ask, 'What happens to the babies?,' for when the babies go, that's the end of us."

She shared another experience in the TLC Nursing Home in Tampa where thirteen black folk are living with AIDS. Underscoring the importance of treating these individuals with respect, she told about the sign on the door of a room of a 21-year-old black man among them. "Please knock as you enter, for this is my home."

Another vignette - this time from Orange County Jail. Seven black women are in jail, and separated from the others, in the back --- isolated and nobody saying anything to them. Her response: "We told them, 'We love you. We're not afraid to touch you.'" Heads that had hung low were raised when Christian compassion spoke in this way.

Mrs. Cousin further reported that in Orlando, white churchmen had commented to her that the black church was reluctant to get involved, but they had never contacted anyone. The Daily Bread Care Center in that city is serviced by the A.M.E. church and the community at large. She also urged that attention be paid to what is happening on college campuses. Students need to know that one in 500 is affected. An issue of concern - at Hampton University, if you test positive, you are sent home.

Mrs. Cousin concluded with the following challenge: "You can do so much. For if we as Christians are truly committed to what Christ would have us to do, to what the Supreme Being would have us to do....The road less travelled may not be the most popular one, but it is the only one I choose to travel if I call myself a follower and a believer. You must be bold, committed, fearless, and you must be ready to take all kinds of criticism. But don't miss an opportunity, not only to save lives, but, as the Africans know, to prepare for the unborn. By so doing all people can live and enjoy what the Supreme Being has placed for us on this earth to which we are entitled beyond the year 2000."

PRESENTATION

"The Status of Health Care for Black Women in the U.S.A."

Julia R. Scott

Ms. Scott gave the seminar participants an overview of Black women's health to determine how and why the AIDS epidemic is all the more deadly in the African American community. She indicated that HIV/AIDS among black women is the number one priority in her organization, which has 150 self-help groups and 2000 members in approximately 26 states who are working on this issue.

Observing that the crisis of health care --- its cost, quality and availability --- is the concern of all people in the nation, Ms. Scott maintained that the United States is facing a health crisis of monumental proportions. Proven prevention strategies are fading. Those who are uninsured, limited insured or permanently uninsurable -- citizens using emergency rooms as their principal source of health care - all are facing diminishing resources.

This crisis all Americans are facing was actually foreshadowed in the African American community. Today African Americans are three decades behind whites in term of life expectancy. Indicators of crisis among African American women abound. Stress is both the cause and the effect of illness. Seventy-one percent of female-headed families living below the poverty line are headed by African American. More than one of four African American women suffer or will suffer from high blood pressure. Chronic hypertension appears to be a factor in up to 30 percent of maternal deaths. In fact, the incidence of hypertension is 82 percent higher among women of color than among white women. A diabetic is likely to be a non-white retired woman living in the city.

Death rates from cancer are soaring in the African American community. Cancer has risen 34 percent for African American women over the past 25 years, compared with 9 percent for white women. Black women are two and one-half times more likely to have cervical cancer, and are much more likely to die of breast cancer.

Infant mortality rates in African American communities resemble those of developing countries. Twenty-five percent to 30 percent of African American women receive little or no prenatal care. Six thousand more black babies die per year than white babies in the same geographical area. Infant mortality is not just a matter of economics either, since the risk of having low weight births is twice as high among middle class blacks as in middle class whites.

Black women are also disproportionately represented among those engaged in substance abuse. Crack cocaine has affected the health of women and infants as no other drug in U.S. history. A recent Florida study revealed moreover that black women are 10 times more likely than white women to be referred for prosecution for substance abuse while pregnant, even though the same percentage of whites and blacks were using drugs.

By 1990, over 200,000 African Americans were infected by AIDS. Fifty-two percent of all women with AIDS are African American. Eighty percent of pediatric AIDS cases are babies born to women of color.

Two-thirds of poor adults are women, and 80 percent of poor in the United States are persons of color, and they are women and children. They are therefore disproportionately represented among recipients hit by budget cuts. The availability of care for Medicaid recipients is declining. Pediatricians who see no patients receiving Medicaid increased from 15 percent to 23 percent from 1979 to 1989 (according to a study published by the American Academy of Pediatrics). Women of color represent over 30 percent of Title X patients. They are three times as likely to rely on Medicaid and, hence, are hit hard by these cuts and trends. We should note at the same time, however, that the full cost of sterilization continues to be covered by Medicaid.

Ms. Scott summarized this discussion by stating: "These are the things we have to understand about our government's policies as we talk about what has to happen to address this issue of AIDS. In most areas of health care, poor women and women of color continue to bear a disproportionate share of the inequities of the system."

Black women also do not always suffer from the same diseases as the majority white population. For example, osteoporosis affects one-half of all white women over the age of 40, but more black women have AIDS, hypertension, diabetes, lung, stomach and esophageal cancer. Fibroid tumors affect 46 percent of black women. Cervical cancer is more common among black women as well. Blacks also have a higher admission rate to mental health outpatient clinics than whites. Finally, according to findings cited in the American Journal of Public Health, the rate of suicide among seniors increased 71 percent among black women, compared with 17 percent among white women.

These statistics lead us to this conclusions: "The single greatest barrier to black women's health is poverty." Blacks are more likely to require health care and less likely to receive it. Further, even when blacks gains access, they are less likely than whites to receive certain surgical, medical and other therapies.

Efforts to bring about equity demand that black women are careful and diligent so as not to focus our attention only on issues facing the majority. Women's organizations have produced a health care agenda. For example, the efforts of the Coalition of Women's Health Research have resulted in a new center at NIH. Their research agenda addresses osteoporosis, but there is less representation of health issues facing black women. Dr. Vivan Penn Wiggins is the new head, a positive choice. Ms. Scott emphasized, "She will have to hear from us."

Turning again to the subject of AIDS, Ms. Scott declared that the AIDS epidemic is the ultimate traumatic burden on an already sagging publicly funded inner city health facility. Nationally, AIDS is one of 10 leading causes of death in women of reproductive age. In New York and New Jersey, AIDS is the number one killer of women of reproductive age who are African American. No other disease in the history of the country has created such a furor as has HIV disease. From the very definition of AIDS to distorted mechanisms of treatment and financing, discrimination prevails. "Until we view this disease as one we all could encounter and

have, and apply appropriate remedies, AIDS will remain an epidemic."

"The time is now", she continued, "for activists to become informed, pressure for improved services and to form a broader vision around this disease."

What happens if her advice is ignored? Ms. Scott painted a grim picture.

> Deeply ingrained societal homophobia, racism, sexism and classism have skewed the public's perception of AIDS and HIV infection. As long as the populations affected are poor, homeless, black, Latino and if the person affected happens to be a women, then her outlook is severe. Her health status is already compromised....On top of that, add the HIV infection and the social stigma behind it, and you have a dead women.

Ms. Scott stated that she was happy to be part of this effort "to engage the black community in this struggle, the real struggle with our own families, friends, homes and churches to change attitudes about who gets AIDS and who is affected by it."

Finally, she reported to the audience the results of a recent poll co-commissioned by the National Council of Negro Women that found that 84 percent of African American women do not believe that they are at risk of contracting AIDS. She concluded: "We have a lot of work ahead of us. It is not enough to listen and to learn. We must go back, teach others and participate in the activism required of us to address the most deadly disease of the 21st century."

PRESENTATION

"The National Perspective of HIV Disease in Black Women"

Frances E. Page

Ms. Page began her presentation by observing that she had been a nurse for 20 years and a health educator for 15 years, and the AIDS/HIV infection "is by far the worst disease I have ever had to encounter in my professional life. There are so many infected and affected by it." She described her mission as getting the workshop participants "to do something." "We have to fight this." She went on to offer the services and support of the National Committee and its National Clearinghouse. "We are committed to help you."

Ms. Page then shared reflections from HIV infected women in the form of several mini-dramas.

► "I was desperate for love. I needed him. Yes, I've had negative things in my life, but I love him."

► "Sometimes I had to do things just to put food on the table, just so my children wouldn't be naked....I'm not proud of what I had to do. I just wanted to survive."

► "'Your test results came back positive'. The most terrible words I ever heard. I was hot, then cold, then numb. It's not fair. It's not me."

All over the world, she continued, AIDS is the number one health crisis in this decade. As of July 1991, reported cases of AIDS totaled 186,895. If you think that for every one AIDS case, there are 50 people who are infected with the virus, this means that in America there are 9,344,750 persons infected and countless others affected by the virus.

Recent statistics reveal that 116,000 adults and 1,600 children have died from AIDS. Women are the fastest growing group of persons with HIV disease. A study conducted by the Center for Disease Control found that 80,000 women of childbearing age are potentially infected and 2,100 babies are born each year with HIV disease.

By 1995, Ms. Page stated, if something doesn't change, HIV will be the leading cause of death for African American women of reproductive age. African American women are nine times more likely to die of AIDS than white women. Black women comprise 12.6 percent of the population of women in the U.S., but 52 percent of the AIDS cases. Ms. Page then asked seminar participants: "What does this mean for the future of our race? HIV disease can potentially wipe us from the face of the earth. Sisters, we need to wake up!"

She went on to address the common response, "'Not in my neighborhood. I don't know anyone infected.' The problem is and always has been that people are afraid to tell, due to the overwhelming prejudice that we created. People don't know their HIV status, and are afraid to get tested."

In reality, AIDS can be found in every state of the union. Surveillance data provided by the Center for Disease Control show that the top 10 states are: New York, California, Florida, Texas, New Jersey, Puerto Rico, Illinois, Pennsylvania, Georgia and Massachusetts. Cities where AIDS is most prevalent, in order of incidence, are: New York, Los Angeles, San Francisco, Miami, Houston, Newark, Chicago, Washington, D.C., Philadelphia, Atlanta and Boston.

Locations where AIDS is least prevalent are: Pacific Islands, U.S., Guam, North Dakota, South Dakota, Wyoming, Montana, Vermont, Virgin Islands, Idaho and Alaska. After asking rhetorically if anyone in the audience came from these areas, Ms. Page went on to compare the rates of potential infection with the number of cases. By way of demonstration, she calculated that even though Anaheim, California reported only 1513 cases, that means that as many as 75,650 persons could be affected. She also reminded the participants that you don't have to have full-blown AIDS to pass it on.

Returning to her initial theme, Ms. Page stated once again that there are people behind these numbers. She made the point: "AIDS attacks human life. There is not a human being alive that is more deserving or less deserving. We are all children of our parents and of God. We're all children affected by AIDS." The issues for women moreover are different. For example, a pregnant woman got positive results and was told to abort the baby. But after 16 months, the little girl she delivered tested negative.

Ms. Page then shared other comments from women infected and affected by AIDS.

- "Sometimes I feel hopeless, but then I think I want to live. I want to stop using drugs, but I need someone to care for me."

- "I've known for two years, but I can't qualify for insurance since I don't have full-blown AIDS."

- "I keep getting reoccurring infections, but I can't get Medicaid. I have a job that pays $800 a month, but I have no health insurance."

- "Too often we are denied services to address the real issues in our lives ---- gender, economics, politics, racism, sexism --- we don't yet have a single voice to advocate for us."

- "We are so preoccupied with meeting the needs of others that there is no time to give attention to our own needs. We simply have to do without the support we need."

- "I know I'm going to die. I don't know when. But until then, I want to have somebody who's going to be there when I turn around and say, 'Help me!'"

Ms. Page's concluding challenge: "Sisters, we need to be there!"

PRESENTATION

"Medical and Clinical Aspects
of HIV Disease"

Dr. Celia J. Maxwell

Introduced as someone "really on the firing line", Dr. Maxwell began her presentation by explaining her purpose and rationale. "I want to tell these ladies the facts. This is something I talk about a lot because I feel very deeply about it. It affects me because I am a woman and I am burying a lot of women in their twenties who could be my children."

She continued: "You know the statistics. AIDS is the leading cause of death of women of reproductive age in New York and New Jersey, among blacks and browns, not white women. AIDS is also (or soon will be) the leading cause of death for these women in this country."

Describing her practice, Dr. Maxwell reported that a growing number of the women she sees are in their forties. "AIDS affects all of us. You can't fell secure. It is not a person; it's a behavior."

Dr. Maxwell then addressed some of the behaviors that are not readily discussed in the African American community. She began by posing the question: "Why is this happening." Black women are not all prostitutes (or rather, sex industry service providers), and they are not doing drugs. (She digressed briefly to explain that the drug at issue is not heroin, but crack with which women - and men - tend to be hypersexual, thus engaging in more sexual activity, which puts the individual at risk.)

There are conditions that facilitate getting the virus, even when such high risk behaviors as prostitution and drug use are not involved. Blood infusions are not much of an issue now, and blood products such as plasma are also safer. It is still true that most AIDS victims have engaged in some form of homosexual activity. That word is not well received in the black community, but that doesn't mean it isn't practiced.

Dr. Maxwell has found in her practice that most of the black men she sees --- who are well-educated, well-dressed, knowledgeable and "doing everything right" --- are bisexual, but they don't tell their partners. (Most white men in her practice, by way of contrast, are almost exclusively homosexual.)

She reported to the workshop participants the finding that was underscored at the most recent AIDS conference in Florence, Italy. HIV infection is now primarily a sexually transmitted disease. Driving the point home, she said: "Forget the mosquito, forget the toilet seat, forget somebody coughing on you....you ain't going to get the HIV virus that way."

Dr. Maxwell then proceeded to describe some of the conditions unique to women that might facilitate or increase the risk of getting infected. Abrasions of the vagina (i.e., like a scrape) is one such condition. They can be caused by chlamydial gonorrhea. Women may protest that they don't get that, but they do

20

get trichomoniasis gardnerella ("yeast infection"). With this condition, if you are in contact with someone with the AIDS virus, your risk has been increased.

Other conditions resulting in increased risk are genital ulcers, syphilis, and herpes. The incidence of syphilis has skyrocketed in the last couple of years, reaching an all time high. Dr. Maxwell is also seeing babies born with congenital syphilis, something she had read about but thought she would never see.

There is also a risk associated with oral contraceptives, which cause the lining of the cervix to get a little irritated, like a scrape. Intercourse during menstrual period can also put women at risk since the broken blood vessels afford the virus easy access into the system. A recent Malawi study investigated why African women using vaginal tightening agents and herbal douches experienced increased risk of infection by the AIDS virus. The conclusion reached was that such douching causes tears and lacerations which again prove vulnerable to the entry of the virus.

Speaking in down-to-earth graphic terms, Dr. Maxwell warned that contact with men with ulcers on their penis, who are uncircumcised and who are HIV positive increases one's risk of contracting the disease. Her advice, "Look before you do anything." She also warned against anal sexual activity, noting that the anus is not strong enough to withstand that kind of friction and increased vulnerability results.

Dr. Maxwell then discussed the symptoms those infected might present. She explained that for the most part, you don't see anything. The disease has a very long incubation period. One gets infected, and might feel sick for a few weeks with symptoms like the flu or mononucleosis, and then one may look and feel fine. "That's the problem," she said. "You look and feel fine and then the risk of transmitting the disease increases."

Once people begin to get sick, the disease manifests differently in women than men. Women get pneumonia but few get Kaposi's sarcoma, which is much more common in men. The average life expectancy for women with AIDS seems much shorter than that for men, possibly because women get to the doctor later.

Women frequently experience vaginal yeast infections (candidiasis). "If the infection is persistent, recurrent and stubborn," she warned, "something should go off in your head." Such infections are common; most women get them when under stress. But if they are resistant to treatment, they may be an indication of AIDS. Cervical dysplasia (abnormal cell changes) has been increasingly reported recently, especially in young women. These women may have also been infected with the human papilloma virus (i.e., "wart virus"), which is the most common viral sexually transmitted disease in the country. (This is beginning to be an epidemic that should also be addressed).

The point is that you can get a "suspicion" of such problems if you have regular PAP smears. Infection with the wart virus and with the AIDS virus makes things worse in the cervical area. This discussion underscores the importance of having regular gynecological examinations.

Dr. Maxwell also addressed pregnancy and AIDS. Pregnancy may make AIDS progress at a faster rate. If a pregnant woman has the virus and gets an infection, it is much worse.

Further, AIDS symptoms are often confused with symptoms of pregnancy.

Yet another possible presentation in women is Pelvic Inflammatory Disease (PID), infection of the internal female reproductive organs. PID is not uncommon and if not treated, could spread up the fallopian tubes and into the uterus. It is frightening in AIDS victims in that those infected with the virus won't have any symptoms. So by the time these individuals get to the doctor, everything is damaged and has to be removed.

These then are ways in which the AIDS virus appears to be different in women. Because there is limited awareness of these differences, women with the virus may have been missed and not diagnosed properly.

At this point Dr. Maxwell outlined various interventions for consideration:

1. Telling young people to abstain is a strategy which was very effective in an earlier time, but according to recent studies, does not work very well today.

2. Reducing the number of sex partners only works if one is in an area where the incidence of AIDS is low. Further, one can be monogamous with a partner who is infected.

3. Having personal knowledge appears to be an effective intervention. If you know you are infected, you are likely to change your behavior.

4. Screening your partners is only minimally effective. According to a study reported in the New England Journal of Medicine that asked a sample of men and women if they would tell the truth about AIDS infection, most women would lie (and even more men would).

5. Peer education seems to work best as far as educational strategies are concerned. A 16-year-old is more effective with another 16-year-old.

6. Condoms can work despite the rumors that they do not fit black men.

7. Nonoxynol-9 is a viricide/spermicide, a type of jelly used with condoms. Dr. Maxwell expressed some reservations, noting that this treatment will kill a virus in test tubes, but "the vagina is not a test tube." Nonoxynol-9 is considered a help, but it will not prevent infection. There have been some reported problems with irritation from the spermicide or from condoms which translate into increased risk. "But N-9 is not going to protect you."

8. Strongly recommended are frequent pap smears, twice a year or at least annually.

Returning to her theme that we are all at risk, and more at risk than we think, she cited the results of a five-year Army study in which the blood of volunteers was tested from 1985 to 1990. Six hundred thirteen enlistees tested positive who had no idea they were positive. Significantly, most of them were black women or teens. Dr. Maxwell also noted that in 1989, the rate of women infected by bisexual men was five times higher for black women than for white men. Further, authors of a recent study that looked at bisexual men in the United States with AIDS found that bisexual men were older (40-50) and twice as likely to report use of mood altering drugs such as alcohol.

Dr. Maxwell concluded her presentation with the following exhortation: "Therefore, as women, we need to take charge. We need to educate ourselves first so we can talk to our

children. We shouldn't hide the facts. It's nonsense that telling kids the facts will lead them into activity. Finally, as black folks, we must remember that we have always had the ability to sort of weather things a bit better than other folks. We must also remember that all of us at some point in our lives will have had a 'skeleton' in our closet, and that the people who live in a glass house, should not be out there throwing stones."

PRESENTATION

"Teaching Strategies for Controversial Health Issues"

Toni Miles-Maloney

Beginning with an exercise that helped workshop participants affirm their oneness (from Louise Hay's You Can Heal Your Life), Ms. Maloney shared the five L's with her listeners as important tools for AIDS prevention education. These are Look, Learn, Listen, Level and Love.

She gave special emphasis to leveling with young people, telling them in her words, "the true truth."

As an example of the techniques she uses with young audiences, Ms. Maloney showed the group items she uses in sex and AIDS education - a condom and sponge. For those who may not have seen either object, she noted that condoms come in colors and flavors (meaning of course that someone is having oral sex). She described the sponge and a "little doughnut" that contains Nonoxynol-9 and suds up when wet. It is inserted into the vagina and then removed with a string.

She explained that when she goes to teach adolescents, she takes items used by girls, such as tampax, sponge and diaphragm and gives it to the boys, to help them determine just how much they really know about female sexuality.

She urged women with granddaughters or even great-granddaughters to become informed so that they can talk with younger members of the family. She advised: "If you don't feel comfortable, go to Essence, other magazines, or pick up information from the doctor and leave it on the bed."

Returning to the final "L", Ms. Maloney spoke about love and gave workshop attendees the charge to be foot-soldiers for AIDS education, involving their churches, Girl Scout troops and bridge clubs. She urged that those present not forget the women who are infected with the virus. Telling of her own experiences, she told the story of a "sister" with AIDS who did not have money to buy sanitary pads, "something most of us take for granted." "She wanted to get her hair done. I gave her some money and took her. That's all it takes. Take somebody to the grocery store, just as somebody took someone's parent in this room when they were old."

She concluded her presentation by emphasizing the importance of networking. "Friends, we are a strong body and we need to pull together to support one another. You just have no idea how strong we really are. And as black women, there is nothing in the world that we cannot do." She stated her willingness to "talk about issues you feel uncomfortable with" and to travel even without honorium if need be, in order to be of service. "I do it because I want to. I have a responsibility. That's my charge in life to do that. And that's your charge also."

24

"A Community-Based Model for HIV Disease Intervention and Prevention"

Rashida L. Hassan

Mrs. Hassan began her presentation by outlining her own approach to the issue. "I don't compare us to anyone" she said. "You will not hear me quote statistics that compare black women with white women, because we are incomparable. This gives you a sense of where I am going and where I have been. Making those kinds of comparisons creates problems for us, problems in figuring out what we need to do for ourselves."

She then shared her experiences of the past week with her 13 year old son, whose encounter with the school system in Philadelphia, complete with stereotypes, "tracking" and low expectations, became a parable for the experience of the black community as a whole with respect to AIDS education.

Urging the audience, "Let us not indulge ourselves in the myths created by other communities that are draped over us," Mrs. Hassan addressed and exploded some of those "myths."

1. "They say, 'The black community does not talk about homosexuality. It is a stigma with them.' But you tell me what black gay men have been relegated to separate neighborhoods? Your sons who are gay come to Thanksgiving dinner, and if they are very good, they bring their lovers. We take them in and embrace them. They sing good on Sunday and they play organ music in our churches."

2. "Over the last 300 years, we have been told that our own sexuality is the problem with our people. 'We are bestial in our behavior. We have no capability of learning and understanding minute scientific information, and therefore there is no point in wasting a lot of dollars trying to educate us.'"

"They are proving it today in Congress," Mrs. Hassan continued. "They have withdrawn a vast amount of money associated with AIDS prevention and education and transferred to client services. If we allow this to happen, they are basically saying that this disease will remain indigenous in our community from time on in. That it will be our problem. But they will take care of all of those infected and dying." Declaring her opposition to this scenario, she said: "I am not going to have it. The class of 1999 is going to walk tall, strong and healthy."

She maintained however that very serious action would be required. Using her own experiences as an example, she shared with the group that she had put her time, effort and career "where my mouth is." In 1985 after having challenged the Center for Disease Control, she returned to Philadelphia and founded BEBASHI (Black Educating Blacks about Sexual Health Issues), which now has a million dollar budget (not necessarily income) and 32 employees. "This means" she added, "we take care of ourselves. We don't ask anyone to co-sign or give us permission for it."

Once more addressing the second myth, she told workshop participants that she flies all over the country telling black communities: "You know how to educate. You know how to prepare and care for people with AIDS. You don't need anyone to tell you that. When neighbors and friends were sick, you brought them soup. When someone was dying, you comforted them. Nobody is doing that for us. Nobody is flying in from Washington to talk to that mother who cannot admit in church that her son is dying of AIDS, but rather says it was cancer or pneumonia. That's our responsibility."

3. There is also a myth that the church won't deal with this issue. Mrs. Hassan told the audience that her first presentation in the Philadelphia community was in a church. The minister told her: "I will pray the opening, but you'll have to talk the rest." But he did give permission for the congregation to hear the message. Calling the attendees' attention to the fact that there are nurses units in every church, missionaries, and other members who can go out to speak, Mrs. Hassan underscored the church's potential to play a bigger role. "Where do people believe people who are dying from AIDS are being taken care of? We talk about it in the church. We are not talking about what they are dying from, but we are taking care of them. And we need to translate that into expanded services."

4. Another myth has to do with the education of our children. Mrs. Hassan's position is that we need to develop better education curricula for our children. She noted that although a lot of people say abstinence cannot be taught in a society in which everything revolves around sex, she recollects that her grandmother had no problem addressing the issue: "Keep your drawers up and your dress down", which truly was a lesson in abstinence.

She also maintained that black adults have to focus on what is good about being a virgin. "Do you believe that it's a good thing at 16 to be a virgin? If so, teach somebody what's so good about it. We need to talk about monogamous relationships and saving oneself for the "M' word."

She moved to another theme: "We must save ourselves." Nothing that everyone cannot "interface with those less fortunate than ourselves," volunteers can fundraise to keep organizations like BEBASHI afloat. She also recognized that the community does not believe the Public Health Service, particularly in light of the Tuskegee experiment. It is clear therefore that "we have to take responsibility for this education. We have to be willing as women to speak out on the issue in our community."

Further, policy makers and legislators need to be approached. Black legislators for example do not understand the AIDS epidemic. Someone has to sit down and say: "I understand what the statistics say, I understand the comparisons, but what it means in the 102nd District of Pennsylvania is this. We have probably more than 100,000 people who are infected with the AIDS virus and don't know it, and 60 percent of them are African American. Or if you know names, sit in the congressman's office and tell him or her that Ms. _____son, daughter or grandchild have AIDS. They have to have it brought home."

"Black people also need to get the attention of the African American media to focus on AIDS as it affects us as a community."

She continued: "We also need prayer vigils and prayer marches, ugly demonstrations, people raising funds, writing proposals and

26

looking at the development of care in the African American cultural context. This means we are not going to send everybody to the hospital because grandma said hospitals are places where people go to die. The alternative for our people is home care."

A further suggestion: "We also need to fight to keep any hospitals left that belong to us from folding up."

In 1985, Mrs. Hassan made a prediction. She forecast that hundreds of thousands of African Americans would have to be lost before the community would be annoyed enough to do something about it. She also predicted that AIDS would be moved to a forefront agenda if women moved it.

Recently, Representative Maxine Waters (D-CA) has stood up in the Congressional Black Caucus and insisted, we will be discussing AIDS. But according to Mrs. Hassan, more is needed.

"You know exactly what you have to do. Each of you knows exactly where you can make an impact on this disease. We are dying in droves. We are distracted because of our socio-economic condition. For some of us, that means we are middle class blacks with a few dollars, but you only live on the periphery of the other black community. You don't go very far. You are segregated and discriminated against. Let us be very clear. We are just like our brothers and sisters, and they desperately need us."

"Come back home," she concluded. "We can deal with our own homelessness, our own poor education. We have Ph.D.'s, M.D.'s ... we have all that we need as a nation, an African American nation, to do something about this epidemic. There is so much to be done that we don't have time to delay. We cannot debate it. We need to just go out and do what has to be done."

It all goes back to Education, Information Sharing and Action. Ms. Hassan's final words: "I hope you will all move to action because I will be coming through, trying hard to keep everyone rolling and moving along."

PRESENTATION

"The Status of AIDS Legislation"

Dr. Leslie R. Wolfe

Introducing herself and the Center for Women Policy Studies as "part of your Washington connection," Dr. Wolfe underscored the points previously made. AIDS is becoming a women's epidemic worldwide and the women most affected are low income women and women of color. She then stated that the social and economic status of women is often ignored in policy discussions about HIV disease. This serves to help explain why women are so much at risk. Imagining all women of every ethnic group and socio-economic status as being passengers in the same boat, and hence all in danger of drowning if the boat sinks, she made the point that all women are affected by sexism. "Therefore," she maintained, "to talk about women and the HIV disease as women in the 90's, we have to make common cause among ourselves in order to be the powerful majority that we truly are."

Noting that most hands were raised when the question was asked earlier in the session as to how many women knew someone who had been infected or died of AIDS, Dr. Wolfe emphasized the point: "All of us are affected by HIV. I was distressed and heartened both to see that nearly all of us have lost people to this disease. And we know we are losing more. And we also know that the Public Health Service lies to us."

She described ways in which sexism affected the treatment of women. She observed that Hippocrates had referred to women's "perpetual infirmities" and asserted that women were associated with illness. "A lot of AIDS education

that goes to women and a lot of research on women has to do with trying to prevent us from infecting men or babies."

She described a recent call about a 12 year-old girl who had been raped by a family member and was now pregnant and HIV positive. Citing this example, Dr. Wolfe maintained: "We are not talking only about women of reproductive age (15-44) or pediatric AIDS. We don't want to stop talking about some of the things that are happening to young women and to girls, as well as to women who are post 44. Not just women "of childbearing age" are at risk. Women over 44 still have a life. "And all of us are at risk."

She explained that the Center has dealt with women's issues since 1972. The organization started with women and violence and added AIDS and women in 1987. Federal policy is an important mission. An important policy issue is the Center for Disease Control (CDC) AIDS case definition. Because women do not present with the same opportunistic infections as men, they are frequently denied presumptive disability benefits by the Social Security Administration (SSA) because SSA is using CDC's limited definition. The CDC definition does not include vaginal infections and gynecological infections. "Why?" She asked the audience. "Because very few men get yeast infections."

The Center's Guide to Resources on Women and AIDS prepared by her organization talks about these issues and also contains a directory of some 350 programs around the country. A video, "Fighting for Our Lives, Women Confronting AIDS" can also be obtained from the Center, which shows eight programs created by women of color around the country who are serving women in their respective communities.

Lessons learned from contact with persons in the field have served to guide the Center's policy reform effort. Until recently, there had been no leadership in the Congress or in the federal government on women and AIDS issues. Now, thanks to the Congressional Caucus on Women's Issues (CCWI), there is a chance to bring about some changes. The real mission underlying these policy reforms is to change the way dollars get spent so that they will be available for work in communities.

Dr. Wolfe then described pending pieces of legislation and urged those in attendance to commit to making their influence felt in Congress.

In July 1990, CCWI introduced the Women's Health Equity Act, legislation drafted by the Center, which was reintroduced by Representative Constance Morella (R-MD) in 1991 in the form of H.R. 1072 and 1073.

The Women and AIDS Outreach and Prevention Act (H.R. 1072) will give funds to health care providers already serving low income women. These clinics, non-profit groups and community-based organizations that are already providing some kind of health care service to low income women should be able to receive the dollars appropriated. Under the Ryan White Care Act, which has substantial funds authorized, this kind of prevention could be funded under Title III for early intervention, but this statute does not mention HIV prevention programs targeted to women.

The second bill, Women and AIDS Research Initiative (H.R. 1073), has as its purpose to require the National Institutes of Health and any other relevant federal agencies to create women-focused AIDS research programs. The research program should develop a much more precise knowledge of: 1) how HIV is transmitted to women; 2) how the disease progresses in women; 3) how physical and chemical barrier methods of HIV prevention can be developed that are controlled by women; and 4) what AIDS symptomatology is unique to women. This kind of research is what the CDC needs to amend its case definition of AIDS. But Dr. Wolfe emphasized that changing the definition should not have to wait. "There needs to be political action to make the change."

Reporting on the status of the legislation, Dr. Wolfe reported that language was included in the NIH appropriation to the effect that the Committee wanted NIH to fund women-focused research. However, that is not yet the legislative mandate required to force NIH to do the right thing. She urged those present to mobilize around the Congressional Black Caucus and the rest of the Congress but also the White House. "It is time to be very powerful about urging the Congress: 'Thou shalt spend these dollars for women.'"

The third bill discussed was the Social Security and SSI AIDS Disability Act of 1991 (H.R. 2299), which had been introduced by Rep. Robert Matsui (D-CA). This bill requires the Social Security Administration to use a different definition of HIV disability, rather than the CDC AIDS case definition. Dr.

29

Wolfe stated that this is the single most important bill being discussed because many women are not eligible immediately for Social Security benefits because they do not have cases of full-blown AIDS as defined on a predominately white male population. For example, a woman disabled by cervical cancer associated with her HIV positive status under this bill would be eligible for her benefits almost immediately.

This bill is likely to move the fastest and needs the greatest amount of support. Hearings are scheduled for the fall, and workshop participants can be notified. Dr. Wolfe added that both Congresspersons Matsui and Morella need additional co-sponsors.

Dr. Wolfe reiterated that all women present are women confronting AIDS. All are affected by AIDS and HIV disease. She reported that she had been told by other women's organizations, "It won't affect our members." So she issued this appeal to the workshop participants: "We want you to be once again, as always, the leaders in moving the issue forward. And when you go back home, don't forget to tell the white women and all of the men of every background, what these issues really mean and what kind of action must be taken locally, at the state level and definitely, within the federal government."

Her final words were both challenging and full of hope: "What has happened is that women, particularly women of color, particularly low income women, have been defined as the problem. We are not the problem; we are the creators of the solution. And we are the ones, with our colleagues on the Hill...who are taking the kind of leadership that will ensure that our federal government joins the communities of women, to fight for our sisters' lives and for our own."

APPENDICES

WORKSHOP PROGRAM

Dr. Dolly D. Adams, National President, Presiding

"BLACK WOMEN IN CRISIS"
Mobilizing Black Women to Prevent and Reduce the Spread of H.I.V. Disease

9:00 A.M. Coffee hour
9:30 A.M. Seminar
Call to Order
Meditation   Dr. Delores L. K. Williams
The Occasion   Attorney Maudine R. Cooper
Introduction of B.W.A. Board &
 National Presidents   Lynnette D. Taylor
Presentation of Moderator   Dr. Bernadine Denning
Introduction of Panel   Ethel James Williams
                                                                        Moderator

Panel Participants

"One Church's Response to AIDS in the Black Community"
 Margaret J. Cousin, Supervisor, Women's Missionary Society, A.M.E.
 Church Program Coordinator, Florida AIDS Stations
"The Status of Health Care for Black Women in the U.S.A."
 Julia Scott, Director, Public Policy/Education Office
 National Black Women's Health Project
"The National Perspective of H.I.V. Disease in Black Women"
 Frances E. Page, MPH, Policy Analyst
 National Commission on AIDS
"Medical and Clinical Aspects of H.I.V. Disease"
 Dr. Celia J. Maxwell, Infectious Disease Specialist,
 Howard University Hospital
"Teaching Strategies for Controversial Health Issues"
 Toni Miles Maloney, BS, Community Program Director, March of Dimes,
 National Capital Area Chapter
"A Community-based Model for H.I.V. Disease Intervention & Prevention"
 Rashidah L. Hassan, RN, CIC-Executive Director, BEBASHI
 (Blacks Educating Blacks about Sexual Health Issues)
"The Status of AIDS Legislation"
 Dr. Leslie Wolfe, Executive Director
 Center for Women Policy Studies

Questions/Answers
Announcements

(Support for this Seminar Provided by the Office of Minority Health,
 U.S., Department of Health and Human Services)

32

BLACK WOMEN'S AGENDA, INC.

WORKSHOP

September 13, 1991
Washington Hilton Hotel
Washington, D.C.
9:00 A.M.
Coffee: 8:30 A.M.

BLACK WOMEN IN CRISIS

Mobilizing Black Women to Prevent and Reduce the Spread of the HIV Disease

AGENDA

"The Status of Health Care for Black Women in the U.S."
Julia R. Scott
Director
Public Policy/Education
Office of the
National Black Women's
Health Project

"The National Perspective of HIV Disease in Black Women"
Francess E. Page, MPH
Policy Analyst
National Commission
on AIDS

"Medical and Clinical Aspects of HIV Disease"
Celia J. Maxwell, MD
Infectious Disease Specialist
Howard University Hospital

"Teaching Strategies for Controversial Health Issues"
Toni Miles Maloney, BS
Community Program Director
March of Dimes,
National Capital Area Chapter

"A Community Based Model for HIV Disease Intervention and Prevention"
Rashidah L. Hassan, RN, CIC
Executive Director
BEBASHI (Blacks Educating Blacks About Sexual Health Issues)

"The Status of AIDS Legislation"
Leslie Wolfe, Ph.D.
Executive Director

Center for Women
Policy Studies

"One Church's Response to AIDS"
Margaret Cousin
Supervisor
Women's Missionary Society,
A.M.E. Church

Mrs. Shirley Robinson Hall
2770 Unicorn Lane, N.W.
Washington, DC 20015
H-(202) 244-1975

Mrs. Gertrude Martin
3675 Gracey Field Lane
Diamond Bar, CA 91765
H-(714) 861-1432

Dr. Marcella Maxwell
35 Prospect Park
Brooklyn, NY 11225
H-(718) 789-5379
W-(212) 306-8405

Atty. June Jeffries
10306 Green Holly Terrace
Silver Spring, MD 20902
H-(301) 681-5270
W-(202) 514-7559

Dr. Marjorie H. Parker
3115 Fessenden St., N.W.
Washington, DC 20008
H-(202) 244-5892

Dr. Marcella Peterson
5104 Glenmoor Drive
West Palm Beach, FL 33409
H-(407) 686-5642
W-(313) 972-1120

Mrs. Beverly Stripling
427 N Street, S.W., Apt. S-605
Washington, DC 20024
H-(202) 479-0455
W-(202) 628-3636

Dr. Elizabeth Stone
1101 S. Arlington Ridge Road
Arlington, VA 22202
H-(703) 521-8194

Mrs. Lynette Taylor
203 Yoakum Parkway #1725
Arlington, VA 22304
H-(703) 751-7131

The Honorable Maxine Waters
House of Representatives
Washington, DC 20515
W-(202) 225-2201

Dr. Margaret Batchelor White
7690 Northern Oaks Court
Springfield, VA 22153
H-(703) 440-9627

Mrs. Delores L. K. Williams
Post Office Box 2624
Indianapolis, IN 46206
H-(317) 283-2511
W-(202) 371-8886

Dr. Lorraine A. Williams
1329 Shepherd Street, N.W.
Washington, DC 20011
H-(202) 882-3072

Dr. Jeffalyn Johnson
10150 Bell Rive #206
Jacksonville, FL 32256
H-(904) 646-9231
W-(904) 646-2710

Mrs. Alexine Jackson
11815 Piney Glen Lane
Potomac, MD 20854
H-(301) 299-5828

Ms. Sonia R. Jarvis, Esq.
1629 K St., N.W., Suite 801
Washington, DC 20006
H-(202) 726-1781
W-(202) 659-4929

HONORARY

Ms. Maya Angelou
3240 Valley Road
Winston-Salem, NC 27106

The Honorable Yvonne B. Burke
W-(213) 253-4439

The Honorable Shirley Chisholm
46 Crestwood Lane
Williamsville, NY 14221

The Honorable Cardiss Collins
400 Madison St., #1508
Alexandria, VA 22314

PARTICIPATING ORGANIZATIONS

ALPHA KAPPA ALPHA SORORITY
5656 S. Stony Island Avenue
Chicago, IL 60637
(312) 684-1282
Rep.   Mrs. Mary Shy Scot
       Supreme Basileus

DELTA SIGMA THETA SORORITY
1707 New Hamphire Avenue, N.W.
WELTAshington, DC 20009
(202) 483-5640
Rep.   Dr. Yvonne Kennedy

JACK AND JILL OF AMERICA, INC.
311 Hawthorne Terrace
Mt. Vernon, NY 10552
Rep.   Mrs. Nellie Thornton
       National President

INTERNATIONAL WOMEN'S
DEPARTMENT OF THE CHURCH OF
GOD IN CRIST
c/o 371 Lynn Haven, S.W.
Atlanta, GA 30310
(404) 775-8674
Rep.   Dr. Lytia R. Howard

IOTA PHI LAMBDA SORORITY, INC.
Post Office Box 11609
Montgomery, AL 36111-0609
Rep.   Dr. Dorethea N. Hornbuckle
       President

NATIONAL ASSOCIATION OF BLACK
WOMEN ATTORNEYS
3711 Macomb Street, N.W.
Suite 4
Washington, DC 20016
(202) 966-9693
Rep.   Mable Haden, Esq.

NATIONAL ASSOCIATION OF
COLORED WOMEN'S CLUBS
5808 16th Street, N.W.
Washington, DC 20011
Rep.   Dr. Delores Harris
       President

NATIONAL ASSOCIATION OF MEDIA
WOMEN
c/o Turner Broadcasting Company
One CNN Center
Atlanta, Georgia 30303
Rep.   Mrs. Xernona Clayton
       President

NATIONAL ASSOCIATION OF NEGRO
BUSINESS AND PROFESSIONAL
WOMEN'S CLUBS
1806 New Hampshire Avenue, N.W.
Washington, DC 20009
(202) 483-4206
Rep.   Ms. Jacqueline Gates
       National President

SIGMA GAMMA RHO SORORITY
8800 S. Stony Island Avenue
Chicago, IL 60617
(312) 873-9000
Rep.   Dr. Katie White
       Grand Basileus

THE LINKS, INC.
1200 Massachusetts Avenue, N.W.
Washington, DC 20005
(202) 842-8686
Rep.   Mrs. Marion E. Sutherland
       National President

THE WOMEN'S AUXILIARY TO THE
NATIONAL BAPTIST CONVENTION
OF AMERICA
4233 College Street
Kansas City, MO 64130
(816) 921-3919
Rep.   Mrs. Lorraine C. Mills
       Corresponding Secretary

WOMEN'S AUXILIARY OF
PROGRESSIVE NATIONAL BAPTIST
CHURCH
537 Woolfolk Street #45
Macon, Georgia 31201
(912) 745-9720
Rep.   Mrs. Earl C. Bryant
       President

WOMEN'S HOME AND OVERSEAS
MISSIONARY SOCIETY OF THE
A.M.E. ZION CHURCH
2565 Linden Avenue
Knoxville, Tennessee 37914
Rep.   Mrs. Grace Holmes
       President

WOMEN'S MISSIONARY COUNCIL OF
THE C.M.E. CHURCH
623 San Fernando Avenue
Berkeley, California 94707
(414) 526-6636
Rep.   Dr. Sylvia Faulk
       National President

WOMEN'S MISSIONARY SOCIETY OF
THE A.M.E. CHURCH
1134 11th Street, N.W.
Washington, DC 20001
(202) 371-8886
Rep.   Mrs. Delores L. K. Williams
       President

ZETA PHI BETA SORORITY, INC.
1734 New Hampshire Avenue, N.W.
Washington, DC 20009
Rep.   Dr. Eunice Thomas
       Grand Basileus

CPSIA information can be obtained
at www.ICGtesting.com
Printed in the USA
BVHW091226281118
534214BV00026B/1521/P